Let's

Get

MARRIED

ROGER H. CROOK

WITHDRAWN
NDSU

Let's
Get
MARRIED

A Manual for Engaged Couples

THE BETHANY PRESS • ST. LOUIS, MO.

210135

COPYRIGHT © 1962 BY THE BETHANY
PRESS LIBRARY OF CONGRESS CATALOG
CARD NO. 62-8758. DISTRIBUTED IN
AUSTRALASIA BY THE AUSTRAL PRINT-
ING AND PUBLISHING COMPANY, MEL-
BOURNE, AND IN CANADA BY THE G. R.
WELCH COMPANY, TORONTO. MANU-
FACTURED IN THE UNITED STATES OF
AMERICA.

BT
706
C7
c.2

To my Students
Who Asked the Questions

Contents

Introduction   9

CHAPTER I: The Meaning of Marriage   11

CHAPTER II: During Your Engagement   22

CHAPTER III: If You Have Doubts   36

CHAPTER IV: Your Marriage and the Law   43

CHAPTER V: Your Conference with Your
                                               Pastor   49

CHAPTER VI: Planning the Ceremony   57

CHAPTER VII: Beginning the Shared Life   66

APPENDIX I: Some Selected Marriage
                                       Ceremonies   75

APPENDIX II: Marriage Laws   95

Introduction

This book was written for young people who are engaged. Its purpose is to help them make preparations for their marriage. Countless premarital conferences with his students and with young people in his church have convinced the author of the need for such a book. As the time for their wedding draws near, Christian young people become aware of their need to have marriage interpreted to them in spiritual terms. They may have had help in looking at courtship in a religious light. In their churches they may have studied the Christian ideal for the family. But during their engagement they find themselves in a very different situation. Since they have gone beyond the stage of courtship to that of planning to be married, their need and their concern are no longer abstract and remote, but immediate and specific. They are looking at marriage with a new sense of urgency. They will not be satisfied with either a sociological study or a purely practical approach. They want to think of their marriage in the light of their Christian faith.

The content of the book has been determined by two things. First, there are a number of questions which the author has been asked over and over again by young people in premarital interviews. Although some of these questions dealt with relatively simple matters, the young people felt the need of answers to them. Other questions were quite profound, probing the depths of the meaning of marriage. All of them had the note of urgency. Second, there are some questions which the author has wished that young people planning to be married would ask. In other words, although the couple have not had the experience which makes certain matters urgent, those matters are nevertheless of utmost importance. The author therefore has tried to give a Christian interpretation not only of marriage itself but also of those details which in our culture are a necessary part of the process of getting married.

The author is indebted to several Raleigh ministers who have read the manuscript and made valuable suggestions: Douglas Aldrich of the Forest Hills Baptist Church, John Brown of the West Raleigh Presbyterian Church, and R. H. Eason of the Westover Methodist Church. A special word of appreciation is due also for the capable secretarial work of Miss Pattie Steen, student assistant in the Department of Religion at Meredith College.

Raleigh, N. C.   ROGER H. CROOK
December 1, 1960

Chapter I

The Meaning
of
Marriage

Unless your experience is radically different from that of most other people, you are discovering that planning to be married is a full-time job. It tends to crowd all other interests out of your mind. Nothing can occupy your time so fully and consume your interests so completely as giving attention to all the details that seem to be necessary for even the simplest wedding. Even though you continue to work eight hours a day, you may find it difficult if not impossible to concentrate on the business at hand. You may try to carry on normal social relations, but everything you do is colored by the coming event. Try as you may to give your undivided attention to work or play, invariably your mind wanders off into that dream world of the future.

Most people realize that marriage is a serious business. There is a consuming thrill, a spirit of romantic abandon, an utter recklessness involved in falling in love, and young people in the process are gay and carefree. But once two people have decided to marry they look at life much more soberly. No one plans to be married with any thought that he might fail in the venture. But neither does any intelligent person assume that success will be automatic. Everyone is determined to find in holy matrimony all that it can offer. Most people realize that it is "the big step" from which, once taken, there is to be no retreat. So serious a matter is it that some persons begin their life together troubled by vague fears and anxiety. They know that to fail in their marriage is to fail in the most meaningful of human experiences. But they know also that to succeed is to find the greatest satisfaction possible in the man-woman relationship and to undergird with the strongest possible bonds all else that is worthwhile in life. Thus wise and conscientious young people plan deliberately and carefully in order that they may be assured of success.

Your marriage will be unique, as is every other marriage. It will bring together one particular man and one particular woman. Since all persons are different, there can be no absolute parallel for any new union. The fact that hundreds of thousands of weddings take place every year is absolutely meaningless to any young couple planning marriage. People fall in love and get married and have children without any regard to the question of where they fit into the larger social order. Marriage and divorce rates, average life expectancy, the average size of the American family, and other such items are simply interesting but irrelevant facts so far as John Doe and Mary Smith are concerned. They do not regard themselves as statistics but as two people in love. The success of their marriage is in no way related to general trends. Neither are they concerned with sociological discussions about the functions of marriage nor theological statements about the divine plan for man and woman. At the moment, they are concerned only that they are in love and want to get married.

Because you are Christian, you need to see that your own marriage is in harmony with the purposes of God from creation. It is the plan of God that "a man leaves his father and his mother and cleaves to his wife" (Genesis 2:24). Jesus quoted this statement with approval (Mark 10:7-8), and so did the apostle Paul (Ephesians 5:31). Although there are some persons who for particular reasons should remain single, marriage is expected of most people because it is a divinely ordained relationship. For the Christian, to be married is to fulfill one of the purposes for which God created him.

It is not by accident, then, that marriage is a universal phenomenon. No human society has yet been discovered in which the institution did not exist in some form. It is one of the givens of life, one of the orders of creation, one of the institutions essential to all society.

The well-nigh universal desire to be married can be understood in the light of the purposes of God. Many persons live meaningful lives without marrying, and some of them deliberately choose to remain single. But most permanently single people did not deliberately choose that way of life. Rather they decided not to marry particular persons because those persons were not considered suitable mates. Some may have made that decision many times, insisting to the end that it is better to remain single than to marry the wrong person. Such choice is not an indication that a person has no desire to marry. It simply means that for him the right person has not come along. But marriage is a normal expectation of most young people, and they spend a lot of time looking for "the right person." This desire for marriage and a family is as natural as the desire for food or for security. People were made this way.

What is marriage like? Since each union is unique, no one can tell you. It is a mystery which can be comprehended only by the experience. Yet, since it is a venture in which so many people engage, it can be described in some general but highly significant terms. From a purely personal and individual point of view, a marriage is essentially a commitment. Two people give themselves to each other without reservation. It is something like the act of faith by which a person commits himself to God. It is both an act of the will and an emotional response. It is the giving of the self with utter abandon. It involves the centering of one's devotion, the surrendering of one's independence, the promising of one's life without reservation. Such is the meaning of the words of the marriage ceremony, "for better, for worse; for richer, for poorer; in sickness and in health."

If marriage is a commitment in the sense in which it has been described, then it can involve only two people. Although there are some religions which permit polygamy, such a practice is utterly out of the question so far as Christians are concerned. It is impossible for one person to commit himself to two others in this way. Such commitment is an exclusive relationship, allowing for no competition. In Christian marriage a man and a woman love each other totally, with their whole being. Such love is impossible of being shared.

This kind of relationship is possible only between equals. It is not surprising that polygamy is practiced only where the dominant religion teaches that woman is inferior to man and that monogamy is required where Christianity is the dominant religion. Of all the major religions of the world today, only Christianity teaches that woman is of equal worth with man. It must be admitted that Christians have not always recognized this equality. Yet the example and the teachings of Jesus make this fact clear and the modern world has been affected by them. Thus, not only is polygamy out of the question, but also the family in which the husband is a sovereign is seen to be out of harmony with the Christian ideal. No person can give himself without reservation to someone who is his inferior. Neither can commitment be a mutual experience where one partner is considered superior to the other.

In Christian marriage a man and a woman are so united that they become one. This unity is neither created by a sudden decision nor imposed by a ceremony. It is an achievement which is accomplished over a long period of time. It is begun during the courtship and strengthened during the engagement. The wedding ceremony plays an important part, though it is not the consummation of the unity but merely one step in the process. Young people in love and anticipating marriage may feel that in spirit they are already one. They may find it difficult to believe that they can ever be more so. Yet in marriage the sense of oneness continues to grow and to become more meaningful with the passing of time. Consequently the time comes when the loss of the mate is really a loss of a part of the self.

From such unity, fidelity is an inevitable consequence. Paul said, "He who loves his wife loves himself" (Ephesians 5:28). A man who is really at one with his wife can no more be unfaithful to her than he can to himself. If the sexual relationship is not an end in itself but is rather an expression of the unity of husband and wife, then the problem of unfaithfulness simply does not arise. There need be no fear on the part of either husband or wife that someone else may steal the affection of the mate. Competition for that affection is simply not a possibility.

This unity has a significant bearing upon the problem of divorce. If two people really become one, then their marriage is indissoluble. The Christian church, following Jesus, teaches that marriage is a permanent relationship. Most church groups recognize that there are occasional circumstances in which divorce apparently is the best possible course, the lesser of two evils between which a couple must choose. Under no circumstances, however, is it the *right* thing. The right thing is the permanent union of one man and one woman. A marriage which is Christian cannot be dissolved, not because there is a church law against the dissolution, but because the union is of such nature that nothing short of death can separate the couple.

Thus far we have discussed the nature of marriage from a personal point of view. There is another aspect, however, which must not be neglected. Although marriage is a personal matter, it is not purely that. Society has a stake in each union. The legal regulations which are designed to protect society will be discussed in a later chapter. Entirely apart from the impersonal institutions of society, however, such as the state, many individuals are directly involved every time a man and a woman become husband and wife. Both persons are already members of families. Marriage does not cut them off from parents, brothers and sisters, cousins, and friends. It is true that the father of the bride "does not lose a daughter but gains a son." Each marriage partner becomes a member of the family of the other.

In spite of all the jokes to the contrary, these enduring family ties are not a curse but a blessing. After you are married, you may draw heavily from your family and your friends in establishing yourselves in your new relationships with one another and within your new status in society. When a person marries, he leaves one recognized status and enters another. Although the change in status involves experiences which are new for him, they are an old story for every married person. The newlyweds take their place alongside the more experienced, learn from them, and share with them in the benefits and the responsibilities of the married state.

Why do people get married? The answer is obvious: they get married because they are in love. For Christian young people this obvious answer has a more profound meaning than it does for others. There are three levels at which a man and a woman may love each other. The first of these is the level of physical attraction. This is the usual starting point of boy-girl relationships. Most people who marry were first attracted to each other at this level. This attraction has its origin in our sexual nature and has a proper place in any successful marriage. Since God created us male and female, it is neither immoral nor something of which to be ashamed. It is essential to a satisfying and enduring marriage. Indeed, many marriages are contracted on this basis alone. Yet, because it is fundamentally an emotional response and because one person can be thus attracted to any number of persons of the opposite sex, love at this first level is not an adequate foundation for an enduring marriage. A marriage based on physical attraction alone will go on the rocks unless the couple advance very rapidly to the next level. It is much better to delay marriage until a more mature love has developed.

The next level of the relationship between a man and a woman is that of companionship, where the two are bound together by shared interests. At this level two people respond to each other as persons. Their response is colored by the sexual element but goes far beyond it. They have a sense of comradeship because they look beyond themselves to some common concerns. They like to be together and to do things together. At this level are found many of the elements essential to a successful marriage. Yet love of this kind also fails to provide a secure foundation for Christian marriage because it is essentially self-centered.

The third level is that at which each person loses himself in devotion to the other. His concern is no longer for what pleasures and satisfactions he gets but for what benefits he can provide the other. He forgets himself as he seeks the very best for the other. He finds his deepest personal satisfaction not in self-seeking but in giving himself to the one whom he loves.

The first two levels of love are preserved in the third, but they are transformed by the consuming concern of each person for the other. Love which reaches this last level governs and directs a person's sexual responses. It gives depth to the sharing of interests and activities. A relationship which does not go beyond the first level can be neither permanent nor exclusive. One which does not go beyond the second remains essentially selfish. But one which has progressed to the third has built into itself the essential requirements for a successful marriage.

People get married because they are in love. Even with a Christian understanding of love, however, this statement does not say quite enough. Marriage is in harmony with God's plan for man. If such is the case, it is not so much the goal toward which a couple move as it is the means by which something of greater significance in human experience is achieved. What is that something?

Insofar as society is concerned, the purpose of marriage is the procreation of the race. It is within families that children are born and reared. This is everywhere true, in primitive cultures and in twentieth-century America. Of course, a small number of children are born out of wedlock, but every such birth shakes the foundation of society. Only where the family is stable can a people be strong. And no provision for the rearing of children outside the home, however necessary such provision may be in some cases, is ever a completely satisfactory substitute for parental care. There is a sense in which people get married in order to have children. Children are expected in every marriage and permanently childless couples are the exception.

In the rearing of children you will find some of your deepest satisfactions. Together you will make provision for the physical, emotional, and spiritual needs of your children. The dependence of your children upon you, their parents, will change into love, and between you and your children there will be that kind of relationship which helps make life really worth while. Our life as human beings finds its significance in relationships with God and with one another. Within the family circle the human relationship is found at its very best.

In marriage you can find true comradeship. A husband and a wife learn to accept each other as they are. Recognizing in each other certain admirable traits, they respond to those traits with genuine appreciation. Recognizing certain faults, they provide help in remedying them. But most of all, they have a relationship in which it is possible for both persons to be themselves, without pretense and without fear. They love each other, not blindly but with full knowledge. Such knowledge is never possible before marriage because it is not the kind that can be communicated by mere conversation. It can come only within the intimacy of a shared life. Yet preparation can be made for it before marriage when the couple have reached the point where they can be completely honest with one another. Such honesty is the indispensable foundation of true comradeship.

Marriage also provides for the fulfillment of the sexual aspect of our human nature. Every person is created a sexual being. Sex is as much a part of our nature as is eating or sleeping. The sexual desire is neither something to be ashamed of nor something to flaunt. Rather it simply must be recognized as a part of our God-given nature.

In marriage, and only in marriage, can the sex drive be adequately and satisfactorily expressed. Certainly sexual intercourse is possible outside marriage. But the extramarital sex relationship rarely if ever rises above the level of merely physical gratification. And if perchance it does involve an emotional commitment between a couple who cannot yet marry, it still falls far short of sexual fulfillment. Only in marriage, where there is the complete giving of the self to the partner, can the deepest meaning of sexual intercourse be experienced. The sex relationship between husband and wife gathers up, symbolizes, and expresses all of those other aspects of their life together which unite them. Never are they so much at one as in this experience. Sexual intercourse outside marriage falls so short of its potential meaning as to constitute a real prostitution of one of God's greatest gifts to mankind. It is for this reason supremely that extramarital intercourse is wrong.

All human relationships are dynamic rather than static. Fairy tales end, "And so they were married and lived happily ever afterward." But marriage is not just one long honeymoon. Nobody could stand it if it were. The relationship between husband and wife does not cease to be happy, but their happiness is of a different kind because it results from a different kind of relationship. As you look toward marriage, your love is characterized by a sense of excitement, romance, thrill. You are preparing to enter a new relationship. You are discovering one another. But in marriage the pattern of your love will change, gradually and imperceptibly. Excitement and thrill may continue, but the security of acceptance will come to dominate. The romantic sense of intimacy will become a sense of unity. The excitement of anticipation will become the calm realization of the best possible in man-woman relationships.

You need not worry about trying to make the change. It is the logical, natural development which takes place in a Christian marriage. Neither should you look upon the change as something to be dreaded, something that comes upon older people against their will. As meaningful as is the romantic relationship between people anticipating marriage, or between newlyweds, that relationship finds its fulfillment in the deepening love of husband and wife after the honeymoon is over.

Chapter II

During Your Engagement

Your engagement may be far more important than you realize. Superficially it appears to be merely a useless and tantalizing waiting period before marriage. Indeed, many young people, and particularly young men, see no point in it. If a couple are in love and intend to marry, why do they have to have an engagement? Why should they postpone their wedding if they are ready for it?

The fact is that you are not likely to be ready to marry when you are ready to become engaged. The purpose of an engagement is to provide time for you to make some specific and necessary adjustments and arrangements. What are they?

First of all, there is the intangible but highly important factor of mental adjustment to the fact of the change in status which you will undergo when you get married. There is a tremendous difference between the relationship of two people during their courtship and their relationship after they have become husband and wife. This difference is not merely physical. It is also a frame of mind. It is closely associated with the change in the love relationship discussed in Chapter One. It does not come quickly nor is it brought about merely by an act of the will. It develops only with the passing of time. Until a couple become engaged, both the man and the woman are still on the marriage market. No matter how much in love they may be, they are not completely committed to one another. They still see other people as potential mates, and they still regard themselves as free.

None of these facts is true of married people. The entire picture is different once the wedding ceremony has been performed. The married person has taken a wife or a husband " 'til death do us part." Henceforth there will be no romantic involvements with other people. There will be continued associations with people of the opposite sex, but they will be very different in character. The adjustment of the mind from the one condition to the other takes time. The engagement helps provide that time.

At its best, this adjustment period is a time of deepening relationships. If it is to be so for you, however, you must be completely frank with one another. This does not mean that you must go into all the details of your past. Anything from the past that might seriously affect your sense of mutuality ought to be brought out into the open during the engagement. Nothing should be permitted to remain a shadow from the past forever haunting the present. Neither of you should ever seek to avoid a frank discussion of anything which the other considers important.

Yet the past is now important only as its affects the present or the future. There is no need to discuss that which has no bearing on your relationship with one another. If no good purpose would be served by discussion, then silence may be the best course to follow. The dominant concern during an engagement is an adequate preparation for marriage. Most of us have things in our past of which we are now ashamed. If a person has come to be sorry for what he has done and has sought God's forgiveness, then he should accept that forgiveness and not permit the past to disrupt the present. For the sake of the marriage there must be no attempt to deceive, but neither must there be any undue exaggeration of the importance of the past.

Far more important than the facts of the past, so far as relationships between people are concerned, are present attitudes, ideals, and ambitions. It is here that frankness and honesty are of overwhelming importance. What a man honestly believes about religion, for example, will have a profound influence upon his relationships with his wife. An understanding of the man's vocational ambitions will help his prospective bride know how she can find contentment and security as his wife. If the girl has any resentments toward her parents or if she is on bad terms with her brothers and sisters, these emotional problems will affect her relationships with her husband.

You need not necessarily have a formal session in which you ask, "Do we really want to marry each other?" You should have asked that question long before you agreed to get married. Rather you should seek through perfect honesty and sincerity to know each other as fully as possible. This is the time for you courageously to discard all pretense. Probably there was some deceit in the courtship, when both of you put your best foot forward. Always there were rivals who might step in and take your place if there were a temporary alienation. You had to be constantly on guard so as not to say anything that might offend. But such cannot be the case now that you have reached the point of planning to be married. Now you must entrust yourselves completely to each other. If you are afraid that such perfect sincerity might alienate you from one another, then perhaps you are not yet ready for marriage. Only honesty and sincerity can establish the kind of relationship upon which an enduring marriage can be built.

Frankness will help you make the transition in your love from romance to sincerity. The mysterious and the unknown hold a delightful attraction—in people as well as in places. During courtship there is the ever-recurring thrill of the discovery of some new facet in the personality of the friend. There is something exhilarating about the establishment of new relationships. By the time a couple become engaged, however, the glamour of the new has begun to disappear. Although no one ever knows all there is to know about anyone, most engaged couples find that their deepest joy comes not from discovery but from security and acceptance. To the romance of the new and exciting is added the security of the familiar and the understood. When this happens to you, you are well on the way to that deepening and strengthening of your relationship which is to be the foundation for an enduring marriage.

Security in marriage is found in the togetherness of a couple, in their sense of acceptance of each other as they are. Courtship is a time of competition. The selection of a marital partner is a real contest with no holds barred. "All's fair in love and war." Men vie with each other for the favor of their chosen girl, and the girls compete with each other no less for the attention of a given man. There is a constant threat of being cut out by someone else. In marriage this competition has ceased; the selection has been made. Both partners know that no one can replace them. Such acceptance is far more satisfying than the uncertainty of romance.

Is this security which is found in marriage characteristic of the engagement as well? Or is competition still a factor to be reckoned with? In a sense there is still a degree of competition, for there is something tentative about the promise to marry. Engagements are sometimes broken. Yet, the element of competition should be eliminated as far as possible. If you are making definite plans for marriage, then neither of you should be involved with a third party in any way that could be interpreted as romantic. The objective of your engagement is compromised if either of you dates someone else. Indeed, if you wish to do so, that desire is a pretty good indication that you are not yet willing to restrict your romantic interests for the rest of your life to one person. In most instances a couple have pretty well stopped dating other people before they finally reach the point of agreeing to be married. During the engagement they should be able to make certain that they can really be satisfied without romantic contacts with other people.

As you become more secure in your love for one another, you may feel a strong desire to become more intimate in your expressions of affection. You need have no sense of guilt in the intensification of the sexual desire because it is preparation for full and free expression in marriage. But you do need to recognize that the strength of the sex drive is such that too much love-making may upset your emotional equilibrium and even override your moral convictions. Much of the literature on the family reveals that an alarmingly large number of couples have intercourse during their engagement. Some of the literature claims that there may be nothing seriously wrong with premarital intercourse because it is so common.

Christian young people are concerned both about hazards which such conduct would create for their approaching marriage and about the violation of Christian standards which it would represent.

What are those hazards? One of the most serious—and surprising—is that rather than binding a couple closer together, premarital intercourse often drives them apart. It does so because it cannot possibly have the full meaning which intercourse has in marriage. Sex is not a biological relationship only. It is a tool, a means of expressing something which is vastly more important than itself. This something is so intimately identified with marriage that the two cannot be separated. It is the essence of oneness, of mutual concern, of the shared life which is simply impossible outside marriage. Even between people who love each other, premarital intercourse must fall short of the best possible in the sex relationship. Because it falls short, it often leaves the couple with a sense of disappointment, frustration, and even estrangement.

This first hazard suggests a second. Between two people who love each other the physical aspect of the sex relationship becomes an important factor. Yet it cannot be said too often that properly understood sex is much more than physical. It is also emotional and spiritual. However much two people may be in love, outside of marriage they simply cannot achieve that emotional and spiritual unity of which sexual intercourse is the expression. To engage in intercourse before marriage is therefore to cheapen the relationship by using it for a lower purpose than that for which it was intended. In marriage it will then be difficult if not impossible to achieve the highest and best of which the relationship is possible.

A third hazard is found in what premarital intercourse implies about the lack of self-control on the part of the persons involved. However strong the desire for intercourse may be, if the couple are not mature enough to control it, then neither are they sufficiently mature for marriage. Even in marriage there cannot be unlimited gratification of the sex desire. Such things as the wife's menstrual period, conditions of health, fatigue, and the like may interfere. A meaningful mutual relationship is dependent upon a high degree of self-control. The person who does not have this quality before marriage may develop it in marriage—but the odds are against him.

Another hazard which cannot be ignored, although for Christians it is not the primary consideration, is the possibility of pregnancy. In spite of recent advances in the development of contraceptive techniques, there is no method now known which is completely safe. At any time a couple engage in sexual intercourse there is a possibility that the woman may become pregnant. Such an eventuality necessitates radical revision of plans. Even if the couple marry immediately they begin their marriage with considerably less than the best prospects for success.

Finally, and perhaps most important from the Christian point of view, is the fact that a couple who engage in sexual intercourse before marriage are violating the Christian ideal. They are therefore guilty of serious sin. They are abusing one of the most valuable of all the gifts of God to them. Even though forgiveness is always available to those who truly repent, the deed cannot be undone. The Christian couple know that premarital intercourse is immoral. They must conduct themselves always in such a way as to avoid endangering their allegiance to the high ideal of chastity before marriage. Such a course is preparation for allegiance to the ideal of fidelity in marriage.

In addition to making the necessary emotional adjustment, you should use your engagement as a time to settle some specific issues. Birth control is one matter on which a decision ought to be made before marriage. The Roman Catholic Church prohibits the use of artificial methods for the control of human fertility on the ground that such methods are immoral. The Roman Church requires assent to its teaching on this matter before it solemnizes any marriage involving a Catholic. Protestants are not of one opinion on the subject. Some consider birth control to be immoral; others are convinced that it is right and necessary. If you and the person you are planning to marry differ on this issue, some agreement must be reached. It cannot be bypassed because you cannot otherwise engage in sexual intercourse in marriage without violating the conscience of one or the other. If you cannot reach some agreement alone, you would do well to seek the counsel of a minister in whom you both have confidence. In any event, the matter should be discussed during the engagement because it cannot be safely assumed that you are in perfect accord.

A second issue on which some decision needs to be made is the economic arrangement. Perhaps the easiest problem to be resolved at this point is whether the wife shall work. Because it is easy, however, it should not be neglected. It is quite possible that you are not as nearly agreed on this point as you assume that you are. It should be decided early in the engagement.

More difficult than the question of whether the wife shall work is the arranging of a co-operative plan for the use of the family income. How will you make decisions about major spending items? Who is to take care of the paying of the family bills? Will you have a joint checking account? Is the wife always to have to ask the husband for money when needed? What kind of insurance program do you need? Answers to these questions worked out in advance may avoid some serious problems later.

A third matter which needs to be settled before the marriage ceremony is the question of church affiliation and loyalty. If the two of you belong to churches of the same denomination, you probably will have no serious problem. Unless there is some reason to change, it could almost be assumed that you will remain within the group of which you are now members. You will still have to decide, however, which local church to join. You should make definite plans to become actively identified with a church in the community in which you are to live. Newly-weds often are so involved in getting adjusted to each other and to their new way of life that they simply neglect the church. But all people need to maintain an active association with a local church. A couple just beginning their marriage could do nothing that would do more to assure the success of their union than to make their church membership together a vital part of their lives.

If the two of you belong to churches of different denominations, you should come to some agreement in advance of the wedding as to what you intend to do. Usually it is better for husband and wife to belong to the same church. The place where you are to live might have something to do with any change of denomination that is made. If you are to live in the husband's home community, for example, it might be well for the wife to unite with his church. If, on the other hand, you are to live in the wife's home town, the man might make the change. If you are to live in a "neutral" town, the decision must be based entirely on other factors. But every effort ought to be made to get together in one church if it is at all possible without doing violence to anyone's convictions.

This suggestion that you get together in your church membership is not intended to mean that denominational beliefs are unimportant. It is entirely possible that a person's belief in the teachings of his denomination is such that he cannot compromise them by joining any other church. A Lutheran husband, for example, might be so convinced of Lutheran doctrine that he simply could not make himself spiritually at home in a Baptist church. If his Baptist wife were equally convinced of the doctrines of her church, then for either to compromise by joining the church of the other might be fraught with grave spiritual problems. For both to compromise their convictions by joining a third church would mean that neither would be satisfied. Under such circumstances, it probably would be better for each to remain in his own church.

Whatever your ultimate decision about church membership, the engagement presents you with an excellent opportunity for spiritual self-examination and growth. It would be a good thing for the two of you to consider together your faith by asking exactly what you do believe and what forms of worship you find meaningful. You might then compare your beliefs with the teachings and practices of your own churches, and with those of other denominations. On that basis you could decide where you would be most at home spiritually. Your final relationship might be with a church to which one of you now belongs, or with one to which neither of you belongs. But it would be in reality a spiritual home in which you could best exercise your faith.

In this connection, it would be well for you to agree about some religious practices to be cultivated in your home. What you have been accustomed to might have some bearing upon what rituals will be observed in your new home. Regardless of your home background, however, you can find important meaning for yourselves and strength for your marriage through such simple rites as returning thanks at meals and reading the Scripture and praying together. Most denominations provide excellent devotional literature which can be used in family worship.

In addition to all these matters relative to your life together, during the engagement you will be making the more immediate plans about the wedding itself. No matter how simple the ceremony, definite plans must be made about the time, the place, and the people who will participate. The more elaborate the ceremony, the more time must be spent on these details. Many a man becomes impatient and wishes that he and his bride-to-be could simply go off somewhere and get married. But most of them triumph over their impatience and co-operate to the fullest in helping make plans for a ceremony which will be a meaningful and memorable experience.

A second specific matter, often overlooked but of tremendous importance, is a thorough physical examination. There are states, of course, in which a medical certificate is required before a license to marry is issued. The chief medical concern in those states, however, is usually freedom from the venereal diseases and from mental incompetency. This is hardly enough for a person who takes marriage seriously. No person anticipating marriage should be satisfied with anything less than a complete physical examination by a competent physician. Such an examination helps a person know fully what are his physical assets and liabilities. If there is a condition that needs some medical attention or that might affect the marital relationship, it should be known. At the examination the bride-to-be might consult the physician about the best contraceptive methods. Rarely does a physical examination alter the plans to marry, but it helps a couple to marry more intelligently.

A third matter of practical concern is the planning of the honeymoon. True, many couples simply get married and start living together without benefit of honeymoon. Yet every newly married couple ought to have some time together, apart from family and friends, and apart from the normal course of work and social life, so that they can begin without outside interference their life together. They ought to go somewhere that other people will pay little attention to them, and where there are no schedules to meet, no unusually difficult circumstances. Their first purpose on the honeymoon is to get the shared life started under the best possible circumstances. Careful planning during the engagement can set the stage for a most successful honeymoon.

The engagement further provides the opportunity to make plans about finances and a place to live. You can take stock of your economic situation to see what kind of living arrangements you can afford. You may have to spend a lot of time searching for a suitable place to live. It may take you a long time to determine what furniture you need and can afford. You will need to plan how to live on your income. If you make such plans together, you will set the pattern for a harmonious economic arrangement for the rest of your lives.

There is yet one other function which the engagement may fulfill. It may give each person the opportunity to become acquainted with his future in-laws. For some this is not a necessary item because they are marrying "the boy next door." But in our mobile society far more people marry into families that are completely unknown to them. Since marriage does not cut one off completely from his parental home, it is tremendously important to make a good adjustment to in-laws. A little visiting before the wedding can clear up a lot of misgivings which they may each have about the other.

It is in the light of the purposes and functions of the engagement that any couple ought to consider the question, How long should the engagement be? Your engagement should be long enough for you to do the things that need to be done. It should be at least that long, but it should not be longer than is necessary. Emotional relationships are not static during an engagement. Every couple looking toward marriage and planning for it become more and more involved in the lives of each other. They are building up to the climax of the wedding. They are being prepared for marriage. Emotional nature is such that one cannot sustain over too long a period this spirit of anticipation and preparation. If the engagement is too short, then the couple are not adequately prepared for marriage. If it is too long, sometimes tensions are built up and the relationship deteriorates.

As to how long the ideal engagement lasts, no one should be foolish enough to try to say. The relationship of the couple at the time they become engaged, how long they knew each other before they became engaged, the economic and educational situation of the prospective marriage partners, and many other factors should all be considered. What is long enough for one couple might be too long for another. Some of the early students of the family said that there was a positive correlation between long engagements and success in marriage—and by "long" they meant two or three years. But those students failed to consider the number of couples who broke their engagement after it had endured for a long time. In most instances a period of six months to a year should

be long enough to achieve the purposes of the engagement and yet not so long that it creates unusual tensions.
Your engagement can be the happiest part of your relationship up to the time of your marriage. It can be a foretaste of that deepest sharing which is possible between husband and wife. It can set the stage for a happy and successful marriage. All of this it can do if it is seen for what it is: a period of preparation.

Chapter III

If You Have Doubts

An engagement is a time of unsurpassed joy because two people who love each other are absorbed in making plans for their life together. Sometimes, however, the shadow of doubt falls across the path of true love. Many a person who has fervently declared his love has later wondered whether he spoke too quickly. Many a person who has promised to marry another has been flooded afterwards with doubts as to whether he ought to go through with it.

Why should doubts arise to plague a person who thought he had made up his mind? Why should a couple who have been so sure of their love that they have begun planning their marriage suddenly become so uncertain that their plans are jeopardized? For one reason, this kind of reaction is characteristic of all people as they deal with any major issue. When a choice has been made, a decision on which the future depends, then a conscientious person invariably wonders whether he has decided wisely. As he made up his mind, he tried to weigh all the arguments pro and con and to arrive at the most logical conclusion.

But after the decision has been made, often there remains a vague shadow of doubt. That doubt can be dispelled only as the consequences of the choice are worked out in life.

All people long for certainty, but sometimes the best they can get is probability, so they choose as wisely as possible and hope for the best. But even as they hope, they also fear. The intensity of the doubt will vary with the person and with the issue at stake. If the choice has the quality of the irrevocable, the doubts are sometimes overwhelming. Few matters are as important as marriage. You should not be surprised, therefore, if doubts arise as the time for your wedding draws near. Although you cannot ignore them, you should not necessarily take them as an indication that you should call off the wedding.

Furthermore, doubts arise in the minds of engaged couples because their emotional relationship fluctuates. Today their feelings may be either more intense or less so than they were yesterday. Although love is not purely emotional, it has a high degree of emotional content, particularly during the courtship and engagement. Thus it is entirely possible for a person to feel closer to his betrothed at one time than at another. So he wonders, *Why don't I feel the same all the time? Can it be that I really am not in love?*

The greater frankness of the engagement period may help account for the rising doubts. Sometimes, with increasing familiarity, the glamour and romance begin to wear off and disillusionment sets in. During courtship people often create an idealized picture of one another. They see no faults in their loved one, but only the perfect mate. But during the engagement they come down to earth and begin to see each other as they really are. If there is too much difference between the dream and the flesh-and-blood reality, the awakening is quite rude. In addition, each person might begin to wonder whether he can live up to the dream picture which the other has created.

Yet another cause of doubt is the sense of uncertainty concerning what the future holds. People are afraid of the unfamiliar. A couple anticipating marriage are looking forward to an experience which is completely new to them. They know that others have married and "lived happily ever afterward." They know in general terms what is to be expected from marriage. Yet for them the experience is to be entirely new. Because it is new, and because the couple know their own limitations better than anyone else does, they are not sure that they will be adequate. Consequently, as the time for the wedding approaches, they may begin to want to postpone it a little longer.

What should you do if you have serious doubts as to whether you want to go through with your wedding? Should you tell the other person about them? On the one hand, if you tell, your affianced might call the wedding off permanently. If you then decide that you want to be married after all, it is too late. Your problem is not that you do not want to be married, but that you are not sure what you want. If your fiancée is understanding and, rather than breaking the engagement, suggests that it be postponed, she may be badly hurt, a consequence to be avoided at almost any cost. If, on the other hand, you simply keep quiet and hope that your doubts will go away, the consequences may be equally undesirable. Eventually you will run out of time. The nearer the time for the wedding comes, the more difficult it is to call a halt to proceedings. To go ahead and marry even though the uncertainty remains is to run the gravest risk of all because it is to fall short of the total commitment demanded in marriage.

Whether any person should try to keep his doubts a secret depends in large measure upon how serious they are. Since everyone has his ups and downs, those doubts which represent simply a temporary questioning should be dealt with by the person himself. There is no occasion for making an issue of them. If, however, doubts persist and perhaps grow, they should by all means be discussed openly. Two people who know each other will find it hard to deceive one another. Usually the one is able to tell when the other is worried. To try to hide such serious doubts may be to contribute to a deterioration of the relationship. One person may be hurt by the knowledge that the other has doubts. But he may be hurt much worse by finding that a barrier has been erected between himself and the one whom he loves without his knowing why and without his being able to do anything about it. It may well be that by working together a couple may be able to handle the doubts which the one has not been able to resolve by himself.

If there are persistent doubts, a minister or some other counselor should be consulted. Only in the most rare instances can a counselor tell anyone what he ought to do. But the fact is that most people cannot face up to serious problems of this nature by trying to handle them alone. They may spend a lot of time worrying without getting at the real nature and cause of the doubt. But as a person seeks to explain his problems to a counselor, he clarifies them in his own mind. With such clarification he is able to deal with them adequately. Furthermore, the counselor can help him see aspects of the problems which he cannot see without such help. The counselor can help explore the courses of action which are open and help anticipate possible consequences.

If you are seriously troubled, it is very important that you look objectively at the content of your doubts. It may well be that your doubts are really questions about yourself. You need to ask yourself, for example, whether you are really ready to assume the responsibilities of marriage. Are you ready to confine your romantic attention to one person for the rest of your life? Are you willing to surrender your concern for yourself to the extent which is necessary in a shared life? Are you willing to think in terms of "we" rather than in terms of "I"? Are you ready to assume the responsibilities of parenthood with which you may be confronted in a year or so? To admit that you are not yet ready for marriage is not necessarily to confess to a deficiency in character or even to immaturity. It is simply to recognize that in your emotional development you are not yet ready for the next stage. On the other hand, as you raise such questions you may conclude that you are ready. You may see your readiness in such a way as would not have been possible had you not honestly examined yourself.

If you are in the throes of doubt, you should also take an objective look at the person to whom you are engaged. Is this the person with whom you want to spend the rest of your life? It will help answer this question if you ask, *Is she the kind of person whom I want to marry? If I do not marry her, will the girl I do marry be somebody like her? Does she have those qualities which I believe to be essential to a good marriage partner?*

Often doubts take the form of the question, *Do I love her enough?* Many people are certain that they are attracted to a person, perhaps even that they love that person. But they are not certain that their love is strong enough to endure the stresses and strains of marriage. This fear, however, simply reflects a misunderstanding of the nature of love. Love is not merely a response to

40

certain desirable qualities in another person. It is partly that, but it is more. It is a regard for another person which endures in spite of certain unlovely qualities which he may have. It is a commitment, an act of the will, as well as an emotion. And it grows with expression. In this sense, love is not a matter of degree; it can never be measured. No one can ever say, "This much is not quite enough for marriage, but that much is." He can never say, "I love this person just a little more than that one, so perhaps I should marry this one." To love is to enter into an exclusive relationship with one other person. If one person loves another, then he need have no fear that he does not love him or her enough.

Sometimes this question is in actuality the unrecognized question, "Does he really love me?" It might be a fear, unrecognized but real, of being unable permanently to hold the love of another. If so, it is the fear that a more intimate knowledge will destroy love, that familiarity really does breed contempt. This fear can be dealt with only by accepting in full faith and confidence the love which the other person offers.

Sometimes a couple who ought not marry each other become engaged. For them, their doubts are a valuable warning signal. Their self-analysis may make it clear that they should call off the wedding. To do so will be a most difficult experience because it will involve admitting both to themselves and to the public that they have made a mistake about a serious matter. But if a mistake has been made, it is far better to rectify it by breaking the engagement than it is to go ahead with a marriage for which the prospects of success are very poor.

Usually, however, this recommended manner of dealing with doubts helps a couple see more clearly that they do love each other and that they ought to go ahead with the wedding. Their hesitation and fears have been brought out into the open and clarified. They see their relationship far more clearly. They are ready to go ahead on a firm foundation. They face the future together with confidence.

What if you have not been able to reach any clear-cut decision? As the appointed day draws near, you begin to realize that you must do something. Should you go ahead and marry in spite of unresolved doubts? Absolutely not! So long as any deep-seated doubt remains in the mind of either person, you should not proceed with plans. It may be embarrassing to postpone the wedding after the date has been set, but the marriage cannot be what it ought to be if the commitment of each to the other is not complete and wholehearted.

A word of caution, however, must be spoken. It is never possible for a couple to return to a former happier state. They cannot go back to that point in the past before any doubts arose. They cannot start all over as if nothing has ever happened. All of our experiences make their mark upon us. Either the relationship will be strengthened by getting the doubts out into the open, or it will be terminated. There can be no neutral ground. When difficulties arise, they must be settled. No matter how they are settled, they affect the relationship. A decision cannot be postponed indefinitely.

To waver on the verge of matrimony is perfectly normal. Only the person who does not understand the seriousness of the matter takes it lightly. The uncertainty must not be ignored because it may be an indication that the wedding should be called off. But it does not necessarily indicate that. If your proposed union is well advised, if you are in love with one another and are ready for marriage, then facing the doubt together will strengthen your unity and prepare you to meet together the other problems that life may hold for you.

Chapter IV

Your Marriage and the Law

There seems to be a lot of red tape attached to getting married. There are certain conditions which every person must meet and certain formalities through which he must go before he is allowed to marry. Once in a great while the regulations cause someone serious inconvenience. Many people wonder whether there is any valid reason why things should be as complicated as they are. Since marriage is a private affair, why should the state have so many regulations? Why should two grown people who want to get married have to secure the permission of the state? What difference does a person's marital status make to the state? Do the regulations serve any worthwhile purpose?

The state is the one comprehensive organization in society. Everyone is subject to its regulations. Unless the state has certain rights of control over the private lives of its subjects, it cannot exist. And if it should cease to exist, there could be no ordered society, no stability to private life, no possibility of community life. The power of the state is not absolute, but limited. In the event of conflict between the law of the state and the demand of God, the duty of the Christian is clear: he must obey God. But where the claims of the state do not interfere with the Christian's responsibility to God, the jurisdiction of the state must be recognized. In its own self-interest, the state has the right to make and enforce laws regulating marriage and the family.

Marriage, sex, and reproduction, the most intimate and personal of all human experiences, always involve other people. They cannot therefore be purely matters of personal choice. In these experiences people must always conduct themselves in a manner which respects the rights of all other people. But no one can be trusted always to consider the welfare of society rather than to follow his own inclinations. The state therefore seeks to provide such regulation of these activities as seems necessary for the protection and welfare of all the people. Citizenship in a democracy involves both freedom and responsibility. Each person has rights, but the right of others can be guaranteed only as life in community is ordered by law.

Furthermore, legal regulation is necessary for the protection of each individual involved in a marriage. Occasionally someone wants to do something which would have serious and undesirable consequences for himself. To allow him to do so would not be right. A person might be willing, for example, to marry someone with a venereal disease. To do so, however, is a highly dangerous undertaking. Regardless of an individual's personal inclinations, the state has not only the right but also the obligation to protect its citizens from their own foolhardiness. Presumably Christians do not need such protection. Yet this protection must be available to all citizens.

Under the Federal Constitution, the right to make laws governing marriage and the family is reserved to the states. The laws with which you will be concerned as you plan your marriage, therefore, are the laws of the state in which you intend to marry. In this country there are fifty different sets of such laws. In the main, these codes are quite similar and permit of some broad generalizations. Yet there is such variety of detail that any person anticipating marriage should familiarize himself with the requirements of the state in which the ceremony is to take place. Although it is not often that a person encounters serious legal difficulty, some inconvenience is not uncommon and baffling obstacles are occasionally encountered.

According to the law, marriage is a contract, an agreement enforceable by law. For such a contract to be valid, the parties must be legally competent, there must be mutual consent, and the marriage must be in a form prescribed by law. Christians do not look upon their marriage simply as a contract, but they may not overlook this aspect of the relationship. Like all other contracts, marriage bestows certain privileges upon the parties involved and imposes upon them certain obligations. These privileges and obligations are usually matters of economics, residence, affection, and normal sex relationships. The Christian does not need the law to remind him of his obligations in these matter nor to see that he fulfills them. Indeed, for the Christian, the contractual nature of marriage is its least important aspect. He has a higher motivation than duty to determine his relationship with his mate. Yet marriage is a contract for him no less than for anyone else. Duty plays an important part in the life of every person. If it is a subordinate role in the Christian life, it is nevertheless important as a basic, minimum standard. Marital partners have duties to one another.

The most effective technique by which the state regulates marriage is the requirement that a license be issued to a couple before they can be married. Usually this license must be secured in the county in which it is to be used. Certain conditions must be met before the couple can get the license. In general, there are two chief considerations in the granting of a license in any state. The first is the matter of age. Since marriage is an adult undertaking, all of the states set a minimum age for marriage. In most states a girl must be at least eighteen and a boy at least twenty-one before they can marry without parental consent. If parental consent is given, most states lower the minimum age to sixteen for girls and eighteen for boys.

The second consideration is the matter of health. Although all states have some requirements about health, there is wide divergence of opinion from state to state as to what conditions are a barrier to marriage. Some states prohibit the marriage of epileptics, some the marriage of persons having tuberculosis in an infectious or advanced stage, some the marriage of persons with any transmissible disease. Some states seek to prevent the marriage of persons who are insane or mentally deficient. An increasing number of states require a medical certificate stating that a person is free of the venereal diseases.

Marriages entered into on the spur of the moment are always hazardous. The law of many states disregards this problem completely. In some places it is possible for a couple who have known each other for less than an hour to be married. The person issuing the license is concerned only that there be no legal impediments, and there are many persons authorized to perform the ceremony—including some ministers—who are concerned only with the fee for the service.

In over half of the states, however, an attempt is made to prevent hasty marriages by requiring that there be a lapse of some time between the application for a license and the performance of the marriage ceremony. In some states a license is not issued until a specified length of time has passed after application has been made. In others the license may be issued upon application, but cannot be used until the specified period of time has lapsed. The duration of the waiting period varies from one day in some states to five days in others.

In addition to these laws which have a bearing upon every marriage contracted in a given jurisdiction, most states have scores of laws which for the majority of people are simply irrelevant. Every state, for example, has laws which are designed to prevent marriage between people who are close relatives. Half of the states have laws which prevent the marriage of persons of different races. Some prohibit the marriage of chronic alcoholics, and some of drug addicts. Such laws may be necessary for the rare, exceptional case. But many of them simply clutter up the books and would be most difficult to justify logically.

Since the state considers marriage a legal contract, it specifies what persons may officiate at the ceremony. In Delaware, Maryland, and West Virginia the ceremony must be performed by a minister of some recognized religious group. In all other states the officiating individual may be either a minister or a designated civil official. If a minister officiates, all that is required by law in most states is that he be recognized as a bona fide minister of his denomination or sect. So far as most churches are concerned, this means that he must be ordained. A few states, however, require that he register or be specially licensed or even be bonded to perform ceremonies.

Nowhere is a particular form or ceremony specified in law. It is required in every jurisdiction that both parties freely and fully consent to the marriage. This regulation is usually assumed to mean that they are neither drunk, nor under the influence of drugs, nor mentally incompetent, so that they can understand the nature and consequences of marriage. The law of most states further requires that the officiating individual declare the couple to be husband and wife. Some states, however, recognize the validity of the Quaker form in which the couple simply stand in the presence of the congregation and exchange vows, without any officer acting as the solemnizing authority. Always the signatures of witnesses and of the officiating individual must be affixed to the license, and the person solemnizing the ceremony is required to report the marriage to the licensing agency.

For a person to be validly married in the eyes of the state the requirements of the law must be met. Those legal standards are quite minimal, the very least that could be expected. The Christian contracting a marriage must be sure that the technicalities are met. The requirements of his faith are so much higher and of so much greater importance than the legal requirements that, if he meets them, the only legal difficulty he might encounter is in terms of the letter of the law, not of the spirit. As a good citizen he must obey the law. As a Christian he gives his allegiance to a standard that is infinitely higher than what the law demands.

Chapter V

Your Conference with
Your Pastor

Your conference with your pastor is an important part of the preparation for your wedding. Many ministers now ask for a premarital interview with every couple whom they are to marry. Many couples both expect and desire it. They may go to the church study or to the pastor's home where the pastor can discuss with them a number of matters pertaining to their marriage. This practice is a far cry from the day when a couple who wanted to marry could simply go to the home of any preacher and have the knot tied.

Not all ministers conduct premarital interviews. Some have no training for such conferences; some see no need for them and have no interest in them. This fact is no reflection on either their ability or their devotion to their work. It is simply an indication that the practice of holding premarital conferences is not universal among ministers. If your pastor does not suggest a conference, then you are not likely to get a great deal of help from him except on the details of planning the ceremony. In such case, should you desire to do so, it would be entirely

49

legitimate for you to seek a conference with some minister whom you know does conduct premarital interviews.

Why should any minister want a conference with a couple planning to be married? Why doesn't he simply go ahead and do what they ask him to do without trying to become involved in their personal affairs? If they love each other and have a license to marry, what more does he need to know?

On a purely legal basis, the minister who marries people without knowing something about them may make himself liable to criminal prosecution. When he marries a couple, he functions as a civil official. If he violates the law, either deliberately or carelessly, by uniting a a couple who cannot lawfully be married, he may be prosecuted. The fact that few ministers have been prosecuted does not alter the fact that he has a legal responsibility. The minister must be assured that all is in order before he performs a ceremony.

You do not, however, ask the minister to officiate at your wedding because he is a civil official. You ask him because he is a minister of the gospel. In most states, a justice of the peace has the legal right to officiate at weddings. But Christians usually are not satisfied with a ceremony which merely meets the requirements of the law. They recognize that marriage is fundamentally a religious matter. They ask a minister to perform the ceremony because they wish him to invoke the blessing of God and of the church upon their union. If he is to do so, he must be sure that he can do so conscientiously.

Although the minister must satisfy his mind on these legal and religious matters, the conference is not an investigation. The minister will not use the interview as a means of prying into your private life. He will not be seeking some reason for refusing to marry you. Rather he will be trying to assist you in your preparation for marriage. You have involved him in your plans by asking him to perform the ceremony. In the conference he will try to make that involvement as helpful as possible. His approach, therefore, will be in terms of a positive and spiritual interpretation of marriage and the family.

During the conference the minister will not lecture, as if to give some final words of advice, some new information that might prove to be the salvation of the marriage. Indeed, he may conduct the interview in such an informal way that you may not even be aware of what it is. He will simply be talking with you as a friend and a spiritual counselor. This conference is a part of his ministry to you as your pastor.

The premarital conference is primarily for your benefit, not for that of the pastor. You will receive help from it because it is designed to minister to you. As you anticipate marriage, you probably are seeking all the help you can find to prepare for success. You have talked with friends, who may have joked with you but who nevertheless have given you some guidance. You may have read some books seeking information of which you have felt the need. You have consulted a physician, asking his advice on matters of health and perhaps on the sexual aspect of marriage. Since marriage is fundamentally a spiritual matter, you might logically turn to your pastor for help in understanding it as such. You would do well to talk with him early in the engagement.

What will the minister discuss? That will depend in large measure upon how well he knows you and upon what your needs are. If he does not know one or the other of you, he may spend some time getting acquainted. If he knows both, he may lead more immediately into the Christian approach to marriage. He may want to talk about some of the matters discussed in this book. He may wish to discuss the meaning of marriage, or the change in the love relationship or relationship to the church. He may make use of a "sex-knowledge inventory" as a guide for a discussion of the sex relationship. He may make some suggestions about such legal matters as insurance and a will. As the conference proceeds, some topic may come up which he will wish to pursue further. If a serious problem comes to light, it may be agreed that additional conferences are needed. Most ministers have no hard-and-fast outline of material to be covered. Rather they keep the conference a very informal kind of relationship.

It is quite possible that there are some things which you should tell the minister of your own volition. If, for example, there are significant religious differences between the two of you, you should say so at the outset. By "significant religious differences" is meant three things. First, there are great and important differences between the three major faiths in America—Protestantism, Catholicism, and Judaism. Second, there are differences in convictions which occur even between people of the same denomination. Third, there is a difference between a convinced Christian and a person who has no religious convictions at all.

Most churches discourage, though they do not prohibit, marriages across the major religious lines. Some ministers object to such marriages so strenuously that they cannot in good conscience perform a ceremony which unites two people of different faiths. There are two reasons for their objections. First of all, mixed marriages are hazardous. A number of studies have revealed that the rate of divorce and desertion in such marriages is from two to three times as high as it is for those which involve people of the same faith. The famous Maryland study, for example, revealed that the divorce and desertion rate in Jewish marriages was 4.6%; in Catholic marriages the rate was 6.4%; and in Protestant marriages it was 6.8%; but in mixed marriages the rate was 15.2%.

Second, mixed marriages always involve danger for the faith of the people involved. In some unions one partner accepts the faith of the other. In many, both partners simply lose contact with their church. Only rarely do both persons maintain a close connection with their own church. Any minister will be seriously concerned about these possibilities.

Although they are concerned about the problems involved, few Protestant ministers refuse to marry persons of different faiths. They know that when the couple approach them they are already in love and have decided to marry. Nothing that the minister can say is likely to change their minds. Indeed, few ministers will even try to dissuade them from their purpose. But pastors know that there are serious problems involved. For the sake of the marriage and for the sake of the faith, they must try to help the couple overcome the difficulties created by the fact of difference. The pastor may be able to help anticipate some of the problems which are likely to arise and thus to help prepare for them. He may help the persons explore the meaning of their faith and arrive at some course of action. He will not approach the problem in terms of judgment and condemnation, but in terms of positive and constructive suggestions.

By and large, the differences that may exist between people of the same faith are ignored by people planning to be married. They assume that since both are Protestants, for example, or perhaps even both members of the same denomination, there will be no significant differences between them. But there is wide variety within

Protestantism as to doctrine and forms of worship. Even within a given denomination there are significant differences. A theologically conservative Presbyterian, for example, may differ from a theologically liberal Presbyterian more than he does from a conservative Baptist. Again, two Disciples of Christ may differ widely on the meaning of baptism. Such differences may prove to be a source of discord between marriage partners. If they are recognized and discussed before marriage, serious difficulty in marriage may be averted. In a premarital conference the pastor may be able to give some guidance in this direction.

The third significant difference is that between a convinced Christian and a person of no religious faith. In such cases there is usually a sort of uneasy truce between the two. The Christian cannot be quite satisfied until his mate is also Christian. Yet he fears to say too much lest he alienate the other—or lest he lay himself open to the criticism that he preaches but does not practice the Christian faith. In this kind of situation the pastor will be concerned about the possibilities of the creation of a Christian home. That there is danger in such a marriage must be recognized by both parties. The pastor can help the couple face up to the problem and prepare for meeting it.

Another possible complicating factor about which the minister should be informed is a previous marriage which has ended in divorce on the part of either one. Many churches have regulations concerning the remarriage of divorced persons by which the pastor must abide. In other churches which have no such regulations the minister nevertheless has certain principles by which he decides whether he can in good conscience perform a particular ceremony. Most churches do permit the remarriage of divorced people under certain conditions. But if a person has failed once, there is reason to be doubly concerned about the possibility of failure in a second union.

The minister may seek to determine to what extent the divorced person now seeking to be married was at fault. It may be that he had certain characteristics which contributed to the failure. If so, the minister will want to know whether this person has recognized his own guilt and has sought God's forgiveness. He will also want to know whether those personal characteristics which contributed to the failure are still present. If they are, they may disrupt the proposed new union. In such case, the minister may be able to give some help in dealing with them. His chief concern will be with discovering what are the prospects for success in the new marriage. Every minister has the right and the duty to refuse to unite in holy matrimony two people whom he believes cannot make a success of their marriage. His judgment about performing the ceremony will be based primarily upon what he sees as the prospects of the proposed new union rather than upon what he discovers about the past failure. In any event, his concern will be with the success of the union, and he will do all that he can to contribute to that success.

Since the minister is interested in the success of your marriage, he may be concerned about anything that comes to light in the conversation which he believes may in the future give rise to difficulty. If he discovers what he considers to be danger signals, he will call attention to them so that you may equip yourselves to deal with them. He may be able to help you understand their nature and source, and perhaps open up possibilities for overcoming them. If, for example, there are such problems as parental disapproval of the marriage, or excessive use of alcoholic beverages, or irresponsibility, or emotional immaturity, the minister may be able to give some help.

On a more positive side, the minister will want to talk about the sacredness of marriage. This kind of interpretation is badly needed because it is so largely neglected. In modern American society we think of marriage as a romantic relationship, as a legal contract, as an economic arrangement, even as a sex relationship. But we are not accustomed to thinking of it in spiritual terms. The minister may therefore talk about how you can find your place as man and wife in the plan and purposes of God. He may talk about what you can do for each other spiritually. He may discuss the relationship of the family to the church. He may talk about the sources of marital unity.

During the conference the minister perhaps will want to interpret the marriage ceremony. If he does so, it will make the wedding itself a much more meaningful service. Unless you have paid particular attention to the words of the ceremony at some time before the wedding takes place you are not likely to know very much about what is being said during the service. The rehearsal does not provide a good time for such interpretation. At that time everyone is concerned about when he is to enter and how fast he is to walk and where he is to stand and all the other matters of form. The proper time for an interpretation of the ceremony is in a conference before the marriage takes place.

The pastor can be of greater help than most people realize as they prepare for their marriage. He can make your wedding ceremony a profound religious experience for you. He can help you begin your marriage with a deep awareness that you are being "made one" by God. He cannot do so, however, if he sees you only at the rehearsal and at the wedding. His conference with you is the means by which he seeks to accomplish these most important results.

Chapter VI

Planning the Ceremony

No wedding is simple. Although many persons begin with the intention of having a simple service, before their plans progress very far things tend to get out of hand. The guest list grows all out of proportion to the original plans. Sometimes the number of attendants is enlarged. Often the decorations first planned seem inadequate. The choice of music develops into a more complicated problem than was anticipated. And with every change the cost seems to mount.

In all your plans for your wedding, as Christian young people you should be guided by one dominant fact: it is to be a religious service, not a show. The lavish display associated with many modern weddings is simply out of keeping with the religious significance of the event. Certainly you will want to be able to look back upon the occasion as the most memorable event of your lives. Since it is so important to you, you want it to be as important as possible to your friends and your families. But this fact must not detract from the religious significance and nature of the service.

To have a Christian wedding in our culture is exceedingly difficult. In the modern world the religious significance of the service usually is completely ignored. Except for the couple who simply elope, the last three or four months before the wedding are filled with almost feverish activity. The attendants are to be chosen and their dresses selected. The guest list has to be prepared and the invitations sent out. Clothes are to be bought and parties to be attended. The physician must be consulted. The license must be bought. There must be a conference with the pastor. Arrangements must be made to have the church decorated. No Christian young people intend to be irreligious about their wedding. Yet in all the furor of urgent activities the religious nature of the whole affair is overlooked.

The wedding is a religious service. When two people marry, they are acting in accordance with God's plan from creation. The Scriptures teach that in marriage a man and a woman are joined together by God. They become "one flesh" through the grace of God. In no Protestant church is marriage considered a sacrament. Yet the presence of the minister as the officiating individual gives a different quality to marriage from what it has when it is contracted before a civil official only. Admittedly your hearts and minds will be absorbed in each other at the ceremony. Yet that absorption must not be allowed to eliminate the consciousness of the presence of God. You are being united by him, and you are in that sense recipients of divine grace. You will stand not merely "in the face of this company"; you will stand also "in the sight of God."

In the light of the religious nature of the wedding, it would seem most appropriate that the ceremony be conducted in the church building. Obviously it can be a meaningful religious service elsewhere. Since God is Spirit, he can be worshiped anywhere. He can hallow a union in the bride's home or in the pastor's study or in any other place just as well as he can in a church sanctuary. Yet the fact that the sanctuary is the place where people are accustomed to worship adds to the spirit of reverence. This holds true both for the elaborate ceremony with the expensive decorations and many attendants and for the simple service where there are no decorations and no attendants.

How elaborate should the wedding be? Because there are so many variable factors, the answer to this question depends entirely upon you. The number of friends whom you want to be present, the amount of money you can afford to spend, the custom in your community and in your church, and what you think is necessary to make the occasion happy and memorable—all these factors must be considered. Some people spend literally thousands of dollars on their wedding; many more spend less than a hundred dollars. It is probably true that the more elaborate the wedding, the more difficult it is to keep it a religious service. That is to say, the more your attention, and that of the spectators, is focused upon the decorations, the attendants, the music, and upon the reception which often follows the ceremony, the more difficult it is to focus your minds and hearts upon the presence of God. The aesthetic demands should be satisfied, but not at the expense of the spiritual.

Normally the choice of the service to be used is left to the minister. There are many forms of the wedding ceremony. Some churches either prescribe or recommend specific forms. Some ministers write their own. Some persons planning marriage request that certain elements be included. In such cases, pastors usually are glad to make any adjustments which will make the service more meaningful to the couple being married. All religious ceremonies, however, whatever their individual variations, have five basic elements. First, the minister makes a statement about the spiritual nature of marriage. Second, the couple exchange their vows in which again the spiritual nature of the union is emphasized. Third, rings are given as symbols of the union. Fourth, the minister prays for the blessing of God upon the union. And finally, the minister declares that the couple are husband and wife. Within this simple framework there is room for great variety.

An important part of the wedding is the music. In most churches the bride is allowed to choose the music to be used, although in the Episcopal church the minister makes the final decision. There is much to be said for the Episcopal practice because, as we have said, the ceremony is a religious service. Few lay people know how to plan such services. At any rate, you should seek the counsel of your pastor and of the organist on this matter, whatever your denomination.

On what basis should the choice of music be made? Except in those instances where the decision is made by the minister or the organist, it is usually based entirely upon the personal preference of the bide. She chooses pieces which she would like to have as a part of her wedding, and there is no other criterion. There is a sense in which she regards the wedding as "her show." She has been looking forward to this day since she was a little girl. She expects it to be the only wedding she will ever have. She feels that she must therefore have everything exactly to her taste. Her choice thus is based upon her general cultural background and upon her associations or experiences which make one piece attractive to her and another unacceptable.

In addition to your personal inclination, three other factors should be considered. First, only good music should be used. To say just what constitutes good music is exceedingly difficult. Yet even the person untrained in music can recognize that some pieces have a quality of beauty and permanence, while others have only the temporary appeal of the "cute." Since marriage is such an important matter, only that music which is worthy of its high and holy nature should be used in the service.

Second, the music should be appropriate. That is to say, the associations which it has in the minds of the hearers should be those connected with marriage *as it is understood by Christians.* There are popular pieces in which either the words or the tune or both are the kind that call to mind nonreligious conceptions of marriage. A song frequently used in weddings, for example, is "I Love You Truly," by Carrie Jacobs Bond. Even less than the music to which they are sung do these words have any religious connotation whatsoever. All such pieces are simply out of place at a Christian wedding. However pleasant they may be in their association, they are not in keeping with the solemn, moving, profoundly important, and spiritual nature of marriage.

On the other hand, there is a wealth of music which is so written that it suggests the highest and best about marriage. Consider, for example, Dorothy F. Gurney's "O Perfect Love":

O perfect Love, all human thought transcending,
Lowly we kneel in prayer before Thy throne,
That theirs may be the love which knows no ending,
Whom Thou forever more dost join in one.

O perfect Life, be Thou their full assurance
Of tender charity and steadfast faith,

Of patient hope, and quiet, brave endurance,
With childlike trust that fears no pain nor death.

Grant them the joy which brightens earthly sorrow;
Grant them the peace which calms all earthly strife,
And to life's day the glorious unknown morrow
That dawns upon eternal love and life.

These words are a most appropriate prayer for a wedding
because they have direct reference to the sacred character
of marriage and because they are God-centered. Such
music will add immeasurably to the meaning of the
occasion.

Third, since the marriage ceremony is a religious service, sacred music would be most suitable. Indeed, in the
Episcopal church it is required that all music which is
sung must come from the hymnal, the prayerbook, or the
Scriptures. There is a proper place for the love songs
which mean much to young couples. That place, however, is not in a worship service. Music which is appropriate for the concert hall, the ballroom, or the mid-
night disc-jockey program cannot be depended upon to
enhance the religious character of a wedding. Since God is
central in all worship services, the music must be directed
toward him. This is true even of a wedding. The music
which is used should aid both the couple being married
and those witnessing the event to center their minds upon
God. It might even be said that almost any music which is
appropriate for a regular worship service is appropriate
for a wedding.

In keeping with the nature of the wedding as a service of worship, no pictures should be taken during the
ceremony. The desire of people to capture on film and
preserve for the future the beauty of the occasion is

quite understandable. Yet it is distracting to have flash bulbs popping and people running around in the aisle as the wedding processional takes place. If pictures of the party in their wedding attire are necessary, it is a simple matter to return to the sanctuary and make them after the service.

Who performs the wedding ceremony? Except under unusual circumstances, it is the pastor of the church in which the service is held. According to time-honored custom, the wedding is held in the home church of the bride. Perhaps this is because most of the other activities associated with the wedding take place in the bride's home community. It is true that you may approach any minister whom you wish to marry you, and that the ceremony can be performed anywhere. But if it is to be a church wedding, then the pastor of the church is the person who will be expected to officiate. If it is to be a home wedding, the normal procedure is still for the local pastor to officiate.

If there are special reasons for desiring that someone other than the pastor of the church officiate, it is permissible to invite him to do so, provided it is done in the proper way. The pastor of the church should be consulted and the reason for wanting the other minister to perform the ceremony should be explained. The pastor then will contact the other minister, not necessarily as a substitute for an invitation from you, but in addition to it. It would be a serious breach of ethics for a minister to officiate at a service in a church of which he is not pastor unless he were invited to do so by the local minister.

If you want to have two ministers participate in the service, is it proper to do so? It is a little unusual, but entirely legitimate. The invitation to the visiting minister should be issued by the pastor, and the visiting minister is said to "assist" the pastor in the service.

Although it is permissible to do so, it is best not to ask a former pastor to return to perform a wedding ceremony. For one thing, it usually involves considerable inconvenience and sometimes considerable expense for him. But more important, he has ceased to be minister of that church and has moved on to another field. Performing marriage ceremonies is one of the functions of the pastor. The validity of the service does not depend upon close ties with the person officiating. It is far better, on this count as on all others, to accept the new minister as pastor in every sense.

How much should the minister be paid for officiating at the service? Most ministers refuse to answer this question, but leave the decision entirely to the discretion of the groom. Indeed, the groom should never ask the minister. If a fee is given, it should simply be handed to the minister, preferably by the best man. An increasingly large number of ministers refuse to accept any wedding fee. They regard this service as a regular part of their pastoral ministry for which they receive a salary from the church. If there are unusual circumstances, such as a ceremony which requires them to travel some considerable distance, they may make an exception to their general rule. But by and large they feel that to receive pay for this service is inconsistent with their concept of rendering a pastoral ministry.

In spite of all the social pressure to the contrary, your wedding ceremony can be made a profound religious experience. If you desire to make it such, you can plan the service accordingly. You can enter joyfully and happily into all your plans for the wedding, hallowing all of them by the knowledge that yours is to be a sacred union. Without your deliberate effort, no minister can make your union "holy" matrimony. But if you choose to make it such, the minister functions as God's agent in bringing into being a union of two persons who love each other. In the final analysis, it is you yourselves who determine the quality of the service which makes you husband and wife.

Chapter VII

Beginning the Shared Life

I pronounce that they are man and wife." When these words at last have been spoken by the minister, you will find yourselves in new roles in life. These are the roles toward which you have been moving and for which you have been making preparations for months. At long last the changed status will be an accomplished fact. The dreams will be fulfilled; the goal will be reached. This is the end toward which you have been looking for so long a time.

This end, of course, is really a beginning. It is that mysterious "happily ever afterward" of the fairy tales. You will be starting a new life. No longer will you simply be young people in love; you will be married people with adult responsibilities. You will settle down to a new routine of work and daily living. You will assume the responsibilities of breadwinning and housekeeping. No longer can you rely upon your parents for guidance and help. Even your roles in church and community will be different. Most important of all, your relationships with one another will be new. You will have to become accustomed to being "Mr. and Mrs." Though you have chosen these new roles deliberately and with high hopes and ideals, it will be somewhat of a shock to realize that the change has actually been effected.

No newlyweds, of course, really expect married life to be just a bed of roses. Everyone knows that there will be cooking and dishwashing and sweeping. Everyone knows that there is an eight-to-five job that leaves the worker sometimes exhausted, sometimes irritable. Everyone realizes that personal desires and interests will sometimes clash. Yet each newlywed couple faces such realities with unshaken confidence that they will be able to handle all adjustments with ease.

As Christian young people, you have every reason for approaching this new venture with such confidence. As you begin the shared life, you will do so with inexhaustible spiritual resources. Your marriage will be a sacred union, a marriage contracted by two people who feel that in this as in all other major affairs of their lives they have been led by God. You know that there are scores of other persons with whom you might have fallen in love and with whom you could have had a successful marriage. But you are convinced that it is in the providence of God that you have fallen in love with each other. You will be joined together by God in a union which will be indissoluble, not because of any law but because of the nature of the union. The sex relationship will make you "one flesh," not by virtue of its physical nature but by virtue of the will of God who made you male and female.

Your marriage will be blessed by the church. You are a part of a Christian community which has helped to mold your characters. Your choice of one another as marriage partners has been made in the light of the ideals which have become yours through the church. Your new status will not be merely a new status in society; it will be also a new status in the church. You may continue to find spiritual resources for your union as you contniue to worship and work with the Christian community.

Your marriage will be sustained by your sense of vocation—your conviction that God is concerned about all of the affairs of your life. Your relationship in marriage will not be simply a relationship with one another. In a real sense you will also be partners with God, co-operating with him in the development of your lives. Thus you may turn to him for guidance, not merely in crises but also in the daily routine.

With such spiritual resources you may face confidently the new venture of marriage. Much has been said about the problems of adjustment which are to be expected. There are many such problems, but in the last resort all the adjustments in personal relationships can be boiled down to one task: learning to think in terms of "we" rather than in terms of "I." It is sometimes easy, sometimes difficult. Some couples have more difficulty than others. Most couples find it easy at times and hard at other times. But as this adjustment is made, the others fall into place.

This is not to suggest that there is anything automatic about the adjustments. Marriage will not sever you from your past. Rather each of you will bring to your marriage all of your experiences, all of your personality characteristics, all of your ideals. These factors help to determine your actions and reactions. However much in love you may be, each of you will have to learn to understand the other. You will have to learn to compromise and to resolve differences. You will have to learn not only to give in to each other but also to come to a mutual conclusion that is not so much a compromise as it is common agreement. In such a process conflict may develop. If it does, you will realize that it does not sever your basic unity. Rather you will understand that in such a union as yours each can speak his piece without fear of damage to your relationship.

Adjustment obviously will be a more prominent factor in the early months of married life than it will be later. Some issues which are likely to come up in the early stages of matrimony are of such nature that they can be settled permanently. Since personal relationships are dynamic rather than static, however, the need for adjustment is a constant factor in all marriages. Between married people there must always be some give and take. Yet when patterns of adjustment have been worked out, specific issues which arise later may be met more easily. The early months of marriage are therefore of greatest importance.

The ultimate objective of mutual adjustment in Christian marriage is the achievement of a sense of sharing. This is a quality which satisfies one of the most basic needs of human life. No one can tolerate being alone. Everyone longs fervently for the sense of being in complete harmony with someone else. In marriage the Christian couple share in joy and in sorrow, in hopes and in fears, in the appreciation of such simple beauty as that of a sunset, in the exploration of a new idea, in concern over the problems of a friend, in the experience of worship. They bare their souls to one another with no sense of shame or fear. They dare to be completely themselves with one another in a world where all other human relationships seem to demand a veneer of pretense and hypocrisy.

It is within the framework of this sense of sharing that Christians regard sexual intercourse in marriage. In no other relationship do two people ever come so close together as in this. Beyond this there is no higher way for one person to give himself to another. For the husband and the wife this is no casual coming together of a male and a female, a temporary experience unrelated to anything else. It is rather the climax and the expression of their total relationship with each other. In sexual intercourse two people who know each other at the deepest possible level commit themselves again to a complete sharing of all of life. The meaningfulness of sexual intercourse will vary in direct proportion to their sense of completeness of sharing in those experiences which are not sexual. Sex on a purely physical level can never be completely satisfying to two people who love each other. If, for example, there is any discord between a couple, they cannot find complete satisfaction in the sex relationship. If, on the other hand, their sense of sharing is complete, it may find its most satisfying expression in sexual intercourse.

People have to learn to share. From the beginning of your marriage you may desire to share in all the experiences of life. Yet the techniques of sharing must be worked out by each couple in their own way. The division of labor, the planning of social life, the spending of money, and all the other details of a common life have to be worked out, often by trial and error. The same is true of sharing in the sex relationship. It is highly doubtful that any couple has ever been completely compatible from the very beginning of their marriage. Each couple has to learn how to make every sexual experience a mutually satisfying one. They must learn also to fit the sex experience into the total pattern of their life together. To achieve these ends may take weeks or months or years. But however long it takes, Christian couples will regard it as a part of the sharing which must be learned.

There is a sense in which marriage is not so much a state as it is a pilgrimage. In it two people cast their lots together for life. For everyone the future is unknown; the married couple face the unknown future together. Wherever they go, they go together. Whatever may be accomplished will be accomplishments of the couple rather than of the individual. If meaning is found in life, it will be found together. Even religious faith, perhaps the most personal of all the elements of life, becomes all tied up with the meaningfulness of one's marriage.

In this pilgrimage of the shared life which you are about to begin you will give full expression to your faith. To share in the experience of worship, both at church and in the privacy of the home, will be a natural desire. It will strengthen your union and will make your faith more significant. To operate on the basis of Christian moral standards in all of the affairs of life will give you a sense of security and permanence. To share in the work of the church will help you realize your vocation—your calling from God to do his will in all things. No marriage can have greater stability and be more meaningful to a couple than the one that has its roots in a loyalty to God which takes precedence even over loyalty to the family.

Appendixes

Appendix I

Some Selected Marriage Ceremonies

1. The Protestant Episcopal Service

The Minister shall say,

Dearly beloved, we are gathered together here in the sight of God, and in the face of this company, to join together this Man and this Woman in holy Matrimony; which is an honorable estate, instituted of God, signifying unto us the mystical union that is betwixt Christ and his Church: which holy estate Christ adorned and beautified with his presence and first miracle that he wrought in Cana of Galilee, and is commended of Saint Paul to be honourable among all men: and therefore is not by any to be entered into unadvisedly or lightly; but reverently, discreetly, advisedly, soberly, and in the fear of God. Into this holy estate these two persons present come now to be joined. If any man can show just cause, why they may not lawfully be joined together, let him now speak, or else hereafter for ever hold his peace.

Speaking unto the Persons who are to be married he shall say,

I require and charge you both, as ye will answer at the dreadful day of judgment when the secrets of all hearts shall be disclosed, that if either of you know any impediment, why ye may not be lawfully joined together in Matrimony, ye do now confess it. For be ye well assured, that if any persons are joined together otherwise than as God's Word doth allow, their marriage is not lawful.

The Minister shall say to the man,

N. wilt thou have this Woman to thy wedded wife, to live together after God's ordinance in the holy estate of Matrimony? Wilt thou love her, comfort her, honour, and keep her in sickness and in health; and, forsaking all others, keep thee only unto her, so long as ye both shall live?

The Man shall answer,

I will.

Then shall the Minister say unto the Woman,

N. wilt thou have this Man to thy wedded husband, to live together after God's ordinance in the holy state of matrimony? Wilt thou love him, comfort him, honour and keep him in sickness and in health; and, forsaking all others, keep thee only unto him, so long as ye both shall live?

The Woman shall answer,

I will.

Then shall the Minister say,

Who giveth this Woman to be married to this Man?

Then shall they give their troth to each other in this manner. The Minister, receiving the Woman at her father's or friend's hands, shall cause the Man with his right hand to take the Woman by her right hand, and to say after him as followeth,

I N. take thee N. to my wedded Wife, to have and to hold from this day forward, for better for worse, for richer for poorer, in sickness and in health, to love and to cherish, till death us do part, according to God's holy ordinance; and thereto I plight thee my troth.

Then shall they loose their hands; and the Woman with her right hand taking the Man by his right hand, shall likewise say after the Minister,

I N. take thee N. to my wedded Husband, to have and to hold from this day forward, for better for worse, for richer for poorer, in sickness and in health, to love and to cherish, till death us do part, according to God's holy ordinance; and thereto I give thee my troth.

Then shall they again loose their hands; and the Man shall give unto the Woman a Ring on this wise: the Minister taking the Ring shall deliver it unto the Man, to put it upon the fourth finger of the Woman's left hand. And the Man holding the Ring there, and taught by the Minister, shall say,

With this Ring I thee wed: In the Name of the Father, and of the Son, and of the Holy Ghost. Amen.

And, before delivering the Ring to the Man, the Minister may say as followeth,

Bless, O Lord, this Ring, that he who gives it and she who wears it may abide in thy peace, and continue in thy favour, unto their life's end; through Jesus Christ our Lord. Amen.

Then, the Man leaving the Ring upon the fourth finger of the Woman's left hand, the Minister shall say,

Let us pray.

Then shall the Minister and the People still standing say the Lord's Prayer.

Our Father, who art in heaven, Hallowed by thy Name. Thy kingdom come. Thy will be done, On earth, As it is in heaven. Give us this day our daily bread. And forgive us our trespasses, As we forgive those who trespass against us. And lead us not into temptation, But deliver us from evil. For thine is the kingdom, and the power, and the glory, for ever and ever. Amen.

Then shall the Minister add,

O Eternal God, Creator and Preserver of all mankind, Giver of all spiritual grace, the Author of everlasting life; Send thy blessing upon these thy servants, this man and this woman, whom we bless in thy Name; that they, living faithfully together, may surely perform and keep the vow and covenant betwixt them made (whereof this Ring given and received is a token and a pledge), and may ever remain in perfect love and peace together, and live according to thy laws; through Jesus Christ our Lord. *Amen.*

Then shall the Minister join their right hands together, and say,

Those whom God hath joined together let no man put asunder.

Then shall the Minister speak unto the company.

Forasmuch as *N.* and *N.* have consented together in holy wedlock, and have witnessed the same before God and this company, and thereto have given and pledged their troth, each to the other, and have declared the same by giving and receiving a Ring, and by joining hands; I pronounce that they are Man and Wife, In the Name of the Father, and of the Son, and of the Holy Ghost. Amen.

The Man and Wife kneeling the Minister shall add this Blessing,

God the Father, God the Son, God the Holy Ghost, bless, preserve, and keep you; the Lord mercifully with his favour look upon you, and fill you with all spiritual benediction and grace; that ye may so live together in this life, that in the world to come ye may have life everlasting. *Amen.*

From *The Book of Common Prayer*

2. The Methodist Service

At the time appointed, the persons to be married—having been qualified according to the law of the state and the standards of the church—standing together facing the minister, the man at the minister's left hand and the woman at the right, the minister shall say:

Dearly beloved, we are gathered here in the sight of God, and in the presence of these witnesses, to join together this man and this woman in holy matrimony; which is an honorable estate, instituted of God, and signifying unto us the mystical union which exists between Christ and his Church; which holy estate Christ adorned and beautified with his presence in Cana of Galilee. It is therefore not to be entered into unadvisedly, but reverently, discreetly, and in the fear of God. Into this holy estate these two persons come now to be joined.

Speaking to the persons to be married, the minister shall say:

I require and charge you both, as you stand in the presence of God, to remember that love and loyalty alone will avail as the foundation of a happy and enduring home. No other human ties are more tender, no other vows more sacred than those you now assume. If these solemn vows be kept inviolate, and if steadfastly you endeavor to do the will of your heavenly Father, your life will be full of joy, and the home which you are establishing will abide in peace.

Then shall the minister say to the man, using his Christian name:

N., wilt thou have this woman to be thy wedded wife, to live together in the holy estate of matrimony? Wilt thou love her, comfort her, honor and keep her, in sickness and in health; and forsaking all other keep thee only unto her, so long as ye both shall live?

I will.

Then shall the minister say to the woman, using her Christian name:

N., wilt thou have this man to be thy wedded husband, to live together in the holy estate of matrimony? Wilt thou love him, comfort him, honor and keep him, in sickness and in health; and forsaking all other keep thee only unto him, so long as ye both shall live?

The woman shall answer:

I will.

Then may the minister say:

Who giveth this woman to be married to this man?

The father of the woman, or whoever giveth her in marriage, shall answer:

I do.

Then the minister (receiving the hand of the woman from her father or other sponsor) shall cause the man with his right hand to take the woman by her right hand, and say after him:

I, N., take thee, N., to be my wedded wife, to have and to hold, from this day forward, for better, for worse, for richer, for poorer, in sickness and in health, to love and to cherish, till death us do part, according to God's holy ordinance; and thereto I plight thee my troth.

Then shall they loose their hands; and the woman, with her right hand taking the man by his right hand, shall say after the minister:

I, N., take thee, N., to be my wedded husband, to have and to hold, from this day forward, for better, for worse, for richer, for poorer, in sickness and in health, to love and to cherish, till death us do part, according to God's holy ordinance; and thereto I plight thee my troth.

Then shall they again loose their hands; and the man may give unto the woman a ring, in this wise: the minister, taking the ring shall say:

The wedding ring is an outward and visible sign of an inward and spiritual grace, signifying unto all the uniting of this man and this woman in holy matrimony, through the Church of Jesus Christ our Lord.

Then the minister may say:
Let us pray.

Bless, O Lord, the giving of this ring, that he who gives it and she who wears it may abide forever in thy peace, and continue in thy favor; through Jesus Christ our Lord. Amen.

The minister shall then deliver the ring to the man to put upon the third finger of the woman's left hand. The man, holding the ring there, shall say after the minister:

In token and pledge of the vow between us made, with this ring I thee wed; in the name of the Father, and of the Son, and of the Holy Spirit. Amen.

In case of a double-ring ceremony, the minister shall deliver the other ring to the woman to put upon the third finger of the man's left hand; and the woman, holding the ring there, shall say after the minister:

In token and pledge of the vow between us made, with this ring I thee wed; in the name of the Father, and of the Son, and of the Holy Spirit. Amen.

Then shall the minister say:
Let us pray.

O eternal God, creator and preserver of all mankind, giver of all spiritual grace, the author of everlasting life; send thy blessing upon this man and this woman, whom we bless in thy name; that they may surely perform and keep the vow and covenant between them made, and may ever remain in perfect love and peace together, and live according to thy laws.

Look graciously upon them, that they may love, honor, and cherish each other, and so live together in faithfulness and patience, in wisdom and true godliness, that their home may be a haven of blessing and a place of peace; through Jesus Christ our Lord. Amen.

Then shall the minister join their right hands together and with his hand on their united hands shall say:

Forasmuch as N. and N. have consented together in holy wedlock, and have witnessed the same before God and this company, and thereto have pledged their troth each to the other, and have declared the same by joining hands (and by giving and receiving *a ring*); I pronounce that they are husband and wife together, in the name of the Father, and of the Son, and of the Holy Spirit. Those whom God hath joined together, let not man put asunder. Amen.

Then, the husband and wife kneeling, the minister shall say:

Let us pray.

Our Father who art in heaven, hallowed be thy name; thy kingdom come; thy will be done on earth as it is in heaven. Give us this day our daily bread. And forgive us our trespasses, as we forgive those who trespass against us. And lead us not into temptation, but deliver us from evil. For thine is the kingdom, and the power, and the glory forever. Amen.

Then shall the minister add this blessing:

God the Father, the Son, and the Holy Spirit, bless, preserve, and keep you; the Lord graciously with his favor look upon you, and so fill you with all spiritual benediction and love that you may so live together in this life that in the world to come you may have life everlasting. Amen.

From *Doctrines and Discipline of the Methodist Church, Paragraph 1917*

3. The Presbyterian U.S.A. Service

When parties present themselves for marriage, the minister shall use the following, or like words:

Dearly beloved, we are assembled here in the presence of God, to join this Man and this Woman in holy marriage; which is instituted of God, regulated by His commandments, blessed by our Lord Jesus Christ, and to be held in honor among all men. Let us therefore reverently remember that God has established and sanctified marriage, for the welfare and happiness of mankind. Our Saviour has declared that a man shall leave his father and mother and cleave unto his wife. By His apostles, He has instructed those who enter into this relation to cherish a mutual esteem and love; to bear with each other's infirmities and weaknesses; to comfort each other in sickness, trouble, and sorrow; in honesty and industry to provide for each other, and for their household, in temporal things; to pray for and encourage each other in the things which pertain to God; and to live together as heirs of the grace of life.

Forasmuch as these two Persons have come hither to be made one in this holy estate, if there be any here present who knows any just cause why they may not lawfully be joined in marriage, I require him now to make it known, or ever after to hold his peace.

Then, speaking unto the Persons who are to be married, the Minister shall say:

I charge you both, before the great God, the Searcher of all hearts, that if either of you know any reason why ye may not lawfully be joined together in marriage, ye do now confess it. For be ye well assured that if any persons are joined together otherwise than as God's Word allows, their union is not blessed by Him.

Then, if no impediment appear, the Minister shall say:

Let us pray.

Almighty and ever-blessed God, whose presence is the happiness of every condition, and whose favor hallows every relation: We beseech Thee to be present and favorable unto these Thy servants, that they may be truly joined in the honorable estate of marriage, in the covenant of their God. As Thou hast brought them together by Thy providence, sanctify them by Thy Spirit, giving them a new frame of heart fit for their new estate; and enrich them with all grace, whereby they may enjoy the comforts, undergo the cares, endure the trials, and perform the duties of life together as becometh Christians, under Thy heavenly guidance and protection; through our Lord Jesus Christ. *Amen.*

Then the Minister, calling the Man by his Christian name, shall say:

N., wilt thou have this Woman to be thy wife, and wilt thou pledge troth to her, in all love and honor, in all duty and service, in all faith and tenderness, to live with her and cherish her, according to the ordinance of God, in the holy bond of marriage?

The Man shall answer:

I will.

Then the Minister, calling the Woman by her Christian name, shall say:

N., wilt thou have this Man to be thy husband, and wilt thou pledge thy troth to him, in all love and honor, in all duty and service, in all faith and tenderness, to live with him and cherish him, according to the ordinance of God, in the holy bond of marriage?

The Woman shall answer:

I will.

84

Then the Minister may say:

Who giveth this Woman to be married to this Man?

Then the Father, or Guardian, or Friend, of the Woman shall put her right hand in the hand of the Minister, who shall cause the Man with his right hand to take the Woman by her right hand and to say after him as follows:

I, N., take thee N.; To be my wedded wife; And I do promise and covenant; Before God and these witnesses; To be thy loving and faithful husband; In plenty and in want; In joy and in sorrow; In sickness and in health; As long as we both shall live.

Then shall they loose their hands; and the Woman, with her right hand taking the Man by his right hand, shall likewise say after the Minister:

I, N., take thee, N.; To be my wedded husband; And I do promise and covenant; Before God and these witnesses; To be thy loving and faithful wife; In plenty and in want; In joy and in sorrow; In sickness and in health; As long as we both shall live.

Then, if a ring be provided, it shall be given to the Minister, who shall return it to the Man, who shall then put it upon the fourth finger of the Woman's left hand, saying after the Minister:

This Ring I give thee; In token and pledge; Of our constant faith; And abiding love.

Then the Minister shall say:

Let us pray.

Most merciful and gracious God, of whom the whole family in heaven and earth is named; Bestow upon these Thy servants the seal of Thine approval, and Thy Fatherly benediction; granting unto them grace to fulfill, with pure and steadfast affection, the vow and covenant between them made. Guide them together, we beseech Thee, in the way of righteousness and peace, that, loving and serving Thee, with one heart and mind, all the days of their life, they may be abundantly enriched with the tokens of Thine everlasting favor, in Jesus Christ our Lord. *Amen.*

Then the Minister and People shall say:

Our Father, who art in heaven; Hallowed be Thy name. Thy kingdom come. Thy will be done; On earth as it is heaven. Give us this day our daily bread. And forgive us our debts; As we forgive our debtors. And lead us not into temptation; But deliver us from evil; For Thine is the kingdom, and the power, and the glory, for ever. Amen.

Then shall the Minister say unto all who are present:

By the authority committed unto me as a Minister of the Church of Christ, I declare that N. and N. are now Husband and Wife, according to the ordinance of God, and the law of the State: in the name of the Father, and of the Son, and of the Holy Spirit. Amen.

Then, causing the Husband and Wife to join their right hands, the Minister shall say:

Whom therefore God hath joined together, let no man put asunder.

It is fitting that the Bride and Groom kneel to receive the Benediction:

The Lord bless you, and keep you: the Lord make his face to shine upon you, and be gracious unto you: the Lord lift up His countenance upon you, and give you peace: both now and in the life everlasting. *Amen.*

From *The Book of Common Worship*
of the Presbyterian Church in the
United States of America.

4. The Presbyterian U.S. Service

The Lord bless you, and keep you: the Lord make his face shine upon you, and be gracious unto you: the Lord lift up his countenance upon you, and give you peace.

If any here present can show just cause why these persons may not lawfully be joined together in marriage, let them now speak, or hereafter forever hold their peace.

Marriage is a divine ordinance instituted for the promotion of man's happiness and the glory of God. The sacredness of the relation is revealed by the fact that the Holy Spirit has selected it as an apt emblem of the union existing between our Lord and his bride, the Church. Hence, beloved friends, take heed to the exhortation of the inspired apostle, "Husbands, love your wives, even as Christ also loved the church, and gave himself for it." "Wives, submit yourselves unto your own husbands as unto the Lord." The happiness contemplated by this union is realized only by those who fully appreciate its sacredness and are faithful in the performance of the mutual obligations growing out of it, and seek daily God's blessing.

And now as you enter into this new relation, consecrated by heaven's benediction and hallowed by all that is tenderest and truest in human affection, I entreat you both to join with me in the prayer that God may bless this union, and sanctify it to the furtherance of your good and to the glory of his most holy name.

The Prayer

Most gracious God, fountain of life and love and joy, look with merciful favor upon these thy servants now to be joined in holy wedlock, and enable them ever to remember and truly keep the vows which they make as they enter into covenant with one another and with thee, in accordance with thy holy Word, through Jesus Christ our Lord. Amen.

The Covenant

Here the parties join their right hands, and the Minister says:

Do you, M., take N., whom you now hold by the hand, to be your lawful and wedded wife, and do you promise in the presence of God and these witnesses to be to her a faithful, loving, and devoted husband, so long as you both shall live?

The man answers,

I do.

Do you, N., take M., whom you hold by the hand, to be your lawful and wedded husband, and do you promise in the presence of God and these witnesses to be to him a faithful, loving, and obedient wife, so long as you both shall live?

The woman answers,

I do.

If a ring is given and received, the Minister shall say:

Let this ring be the token of your plighted faith, and the memorial of your mutual and unending love.

Then the Minister, addressing himself to the company present, says:

Forasmuch as these persons have covenanted together in marriage in accordance with the laws of the state, I do now pronounce them husband and wife, after the ordinance of God. Whom, therefore, God hath joined together, let no man put asunder.

The Prayer

Almighty and ever blessed God, our heavenly Father, place the seal of thy loving approval upon the union of these two hearts and lives in the sacred bonds of matrimony. Enable thy servants, by the gift of thy sufficient grace, to be faithful in keeping the vows they have now assumed. Whether in prosperity or in adversity, in sickness or in health, in sorrow or in joy, may their love and sympathy for each other never fail. Into thy holy keeping we now commit them, praying that they may ever live "as being heirs together of the grace of life." For Jesus' sake. Amen.

Benediction

Then the married pair standing, or kneeling, the Minister shall pronounce the benediction:

God the Father, God the Son, God the Holy Ghost, bless, preserve, and keep you; the Lord mercifully with his favor look upon you, and so fill you with his grace that you may live faithfully together in this life, and in the world to come may have life everlasting. Amen.

> From *The Book of Church Order of the Presbyterian Church in the United States.*

5. A Lutheran Service

The Congregation shall stand for the Invocation.
The persons to be married having presented themselves at the entrance to the Chancel, or before the Altar, the Man to the right of the Woman, the Minister shall say:

In the Name of the Father, and of the Son, and of the Holy Ghost. Amen.

Dearly Beloved: Forasmuch as Marriage is a holy estate, ordained of God, and to be held in honor by all, it becometh those who enter therein to weigh, with reverent minds, what the Word of

God teacheth concerning it:

The Lord God said:

It is not good that the man should be alone; I will make him an helpmeet for him.

Our Lord Jesus Christ said:

Have you not read that He which made them at the beginning made them male and female, and said, For this cause shall a man leave father and mother, and shall cleave to his wife, and they twain shall be one flesh? Wherefore, they are no more twain, but one flesh. What therefore God hath joined together, let not man put asunder.

Then shall he read one or both of the following Lections:

The Apostle Paul, speaking by the Holy Spirit, saith: Husbands, love your wives, even as Christ also loved the Church, and gave himself for it. He that loveth his wife, loveth himself; for no man ever yet hated his own flesh, but nourisheth it, even as the

Lord the Church. Wives, submit yourselves unto your own husbands, as unto the Lord; for the husband is the head of the wife, even as Christ is the Head of the Church.

The Apostle Peter, speaking by the Holy Spirit, saith: Ye wives, let your adorning be the ornament of a meek and quiet spirit, which is, in the sight of God, of great price. Likewise, ye husbands, dwell with them according to knowledge, giving honor unto the wife as unto the weaker vessel and as being heirs together of the grace of life.

Then shall the Minister say:

Into this holy estate this Man and this Woman come now to be united. If any one, therefore, can show just cause why they may not be lawfully joined together, let him now speak, or else forever hold his peace.

Then shall the Minister say to the Man:

N., wilt thou have this Woman to thy wedded wife, to live together after God's ordinance in the holy estate of Matrimony? Wilt thou love her, comfort her, honor and keep her in sickness and in health, and, forsaking all others, keep thee only unto her, so long as ye both shall live?

The Man shall say:

I will.

Then shall the Minister say to the Woman:

N., wilt thou have this Man to thy wedded husband, to live together after God's ordinance in the holy estate of Matrimony? Wilt thou love him, comfort him, honor and keep him in sickness and in health, and, forsaking all others, keep thee only unto him, so long as ye both shall live?

The Woman shall say:

I will.

If the Woman be given in Marriage, the Minister shall say:

Who giveth this Woman to be married to this Man?

The man shall take the right hand of the Woman and say after the Minister:

I, N., take thee, N., to my wedded wife, to have and to hold from this day forward, for better for worse, for richer for poorer, in sickness and in health, to love and to cherish, till death us do part, according to God's holy ordinance; and thereto I plight thee my troth.

Then shall the Woman, in like manner, say after the Minister:

I, N., take thee, N., to my wedded husband, to have and to hold from this day forward, for better for worse, for richer for poorer, in sickness and in health, to love and to cherish, till death us do part, according to God's holy ordinance; and thereto I plight thee my troth.

If the wedding Ring be used, the Minister shall now receive it and give it to the Man to put on the fourth finger of the Woman's left hand. Then shall the Man say, or if two rings be used, the Man and the Woman, in turn, shall say, after the Minister:

Receive this ring as a token of wedded love and troth.

Then shall the Minister say:

Join your right hands.

Then shall the Minister lay his right hand upon their hands and say:

Forasmuch as N. and N. have consented together in holy wedlock, and have declared the same before God and in the presence of this company, I pronounce them Man and Wife: In the Name of the Father and of the Son and of the Holy Ghost. Amen.

What God hath joined together, let not man put asunder.

Then may they kneel, and the Minister shall bless them, saying:

The Lord God, who created our first parents and sanctified their union in Marriage: Sanctify and bless you, that ye may please him both in body and soul, and live together in holy love unto life's end. Amen.

Then shall the Minister say:

Let us pray. Almighty and most merciful God, who hast now united this Man and this Woman in the holy estate of Matrimony: Grant them grace to live therein according to thy holy Word; strengthen them in constant fidelity and true affection toward each other; sustain and defend them amidst all trials and temptations; and help them so to pass through this world in faith toward thee, in communion with thy holy Church, and in loving service one of the other, that they may enjoy forever thy heavenly benediction; through Jesus Christ, thy Son, our Lord, who liveth and reigneth with thee and the Holy Ghost, one God, world without end. Amen.

The Minister may add one or both of the following prayers:

O Almighty God, Creator of mankind, who only art the wellspring of life: Bestow upon these thy servants, if it be thy will, the gift and heritage of children; and grant that they may see their children brought up in thy faith and fear, to the honor and glory of thy Name; through Jesus Christ our Lord. Amen.

O God, who art our dwelling-place in all generations: Look with favor upon the homes of our land; enfold husbands and wives, parents and children, in the bonds of thy pure love; and so bless our homes, that they may be a shelter for the defenseless, a bulwark for the tempted, a resting-place for the weary, and a foretaste of our eternal home in thee; through Jesus Christ our Lord. Amen.

Then shall all say:

Our Father. . . .

Then shall the Minister say the Benediction:

The Lord bless thee and keep thee. The Lord make his face shine upon thee, and be gracious unto thee. The Lord lift up his countenance upon thee, and give thee peace. Amen.

Or,

God Almighty send you his light and truth to keep you all the days of your life. The hand of God protect you; his holy Angels accompany you. God the Father, God the Son, and God the Holy Ghost, cause his grace to be mighty upon you. Amen.

—From *Service Book and Hymnal of the Lutheran Church in America*

Appendix II

Marriage Laws[1]

State	With Consent Men	With Consent Women	Without Consent Men	Without Consent Women	Blood Test	Wait for License	Wait after License	License Fee
Alabama	17	14	21	18	Yes	None	None	$2.00
Alaska	18	16	21	18	Yes	3 days	None	2.50
Arizona	18	16	21	18	Yes	None	None	2.00
Arkansas	18	16	21	18	Yes	3 days	None	3.00
California	18	16	21	18	Yes	None	None	2.00
Colorado	16	16	21	18	Yes	None	None	3.00
Connecticut	16	16	21	21	Yes	4 days	None	2.00
Delaware	18	16	21	18	Yes	None	(a)	3.00
Dist. of Col.	18	16	21	18	No	3 days	None	(b)
Florida	18	16	21	21	Yes	3 days	None	3.00
Georgia	17	14	21	18	Yes	5 days	None	5.00
Hawaii	18	16	20	20	Yes	3 days	None	5.00
Idaho	15	15	18	18	Yes	None	None	3.00
Illinois	18	16	21	18	Yes	None	None	(c)
Indiana	18	16	21	18	Yes	3 days	None	5.00
Iowa	16	14	21	18	Yes	None	None	3.00
Kansas	18	16	21	18	Yes	3 days	None	(d)
Kentucky	16	14	21	21	Yes	3 days	None	6.00
Louisiana	18	16	21	21	Yes	None	3 days	2.00
Maine	16	16	21	18	Yes	5 days	None	2.00
Maryland	18	16	21	18	No	2 days	None	(e)
Massachusetts	18	16	21	18	Yes	3 days	None	2.00
Michigan	18	16	18	18	Yes	3 days	None	2.00
Minnesota	18	16	21	18	No	5 days	None	5.00
Mississippi	17	15	21	21	Yes	3 days	None	3.00
Missouri	15	15	21	18	Yes	3 days	None	2.55
Montana	18	16	21	18	Yes	None	None	2.25
Nebraska	18	16	21	21	Yes	None	None	2.00
Nevada	18	16	21	18	No	None	None	5.00
New Hampshire	14	13	20	18	Yes	5 days	None	3.00

[1]Adapted from the chart in *The World Almanac*, 1961, p. 456.

95

New Jersey	18	16	21	18	Yes	3 days	None	3.00
New Mexico	18	16	21	18	Yes	None	None	5.00
New York	16	14	21	18	Yes	None	2 days	2.00
North Carolina	16	16	18	18	Yes	None	None	5.00
North Dakota	18	15	21	18	Yes	None	None	1.00
Ohio	18	16	21	21	Yes	5 days	None	2.15
Oklahoma	18	15	21	18	Yes	None	None	3.00
Oregon	18	15	21	18	Yes	3 days	None	3.00
Pennsylvania	16	16	21	21	Yes	3 days	None	3.00
Rhode Island	18	16	21	21	Yes	6 days	None	2.00
South Carolina	16	14	18	18	No	2 days	None	2.00
South Dakota	18	15	21	18	Yes	None	None	2.50
Tennessee	16	16	21	18	Yes	3 days	None	2.00
Texas	16	14	21	18	Yes	None	None	3.00
Utah	16	14	21	18	Yes	None	None	2.50
Vermont	18	16	21	18	Yes	None	5 days	3.00
Virginia	18	16	21	21	Yes	None	None	4.00
Washington	15	15	21	18	(g)	3 days	None	5.00
West Virginia	18	16	21	21	Yes	3 days	None	2.00
Wisconsin	18	16	21	18	Yes	5 days	None	1.50
Wyoming	18	16	21	21	Yes	None	None	2.00

(a) 24 hours if one or both parties resident of state; 96 hours if both parties are nonresidents.
(b) 50¢ to file; $2.00 when license is issued
(c) Cook County $5.00; balance of state, $3.00.
(d) $2.50 for license, plus $1.00 registration fee.
(e) $3 to $6 depending upon county.
(f) None, but a medical certificate is required.
(g) None, but male must file affidavit.